My Life with the Triune God

My Life with the Triune God

BARRIE BREACH

To order additional copies of this book, contact:
Xlibris
0-800-443-678
www.Xlibris.co.nz
Orders@Xlibris.co.nz
724331

My name is Barrie Breach. I am writing of experiences of my life to date, at the request of Jesus Christ whom I have heard speaking directly to me often enough that I am now able to even recognise the tone of His voice. This book fulfills my promise to Him. For a number of years I had thought these interactions I have enjoyed were private to me alone. Now my life is being made public, so that you may follow God's will for our future.

This is as complete an experience that I can recall and in an attempt to tell everything to satisfy my promise to Christ, neither adding, nor leaving out any information about my experiences that I have been privileged to have with one or other of the three persons of The Trinity, with my own thoughts added that I considered God wanted me to say to you my readers.

Christ came to me with the express wish that I should write it all down for you to see including things I had previously considered private. It has taken many attempts to get it right, and if it were not for The Rev. Yvonne McLean, I may never have completed this work.

I am just a normal human filled with The Holy Spirit, and with an unique experience of each of the three persons of The Trinity.

My story of the truth starts, as Christ told me, with my birth. How The Father gave the soul of an angel into a newly born child with two normal human parents. Each had a family of strong Christian beliefs within a church that held to biblical prayers. I have taken what Christ has told me of my relationship with The Trinity God, in order that you might see and have the courage to learn and to take the next step towards accepting the closeness that God has chosen for us all to enjoy and not be afraid to find the love and intermitency, that God wishes for all His people, which includes you.

The period before my birth relies on the words of Christ as He told them to me. It all appeared to me to be so outrageous, that first I thought Christ was teasing me, for He was happy and in a jovial mood. I did not therefore take Him all that serious, until The Father came to Jesus' rescue, and the shock made me fall off the corner of my bed. You will read about the details of that later.

I was born in September 1937, just two years before the second world war. The Father had put a great deal of thought into His decision, and did not want His work destroyed. Therefore He chose my birthplace would be as far away from war activities as possible, into a family attending a church which did not honour some members above others, but allowed God the right to retain that activity.

With my mother's pregnancy was already established, and having recently arrived in Christchurch New Zealand, God could see the selection was an easy choice for Him. The angel in question had for a long period accepted God's decision.

Like all children, I had nightmares, mostly about the war, which I did not understand. I always tried to levitate above it all, if only my powers of thought were strong enough. I know of no other child who tried to escape this way. I put the experience down to the fact that I had a soul of an angel, and in my subconsciousness, levitation was normal. Perhaps I am wrong in my assumption; yet it seemed feasible to me.

At seven years of age, I awoke early one Sunday. It was still twilight, and I saw two guarding angels in the open doorway into my bedroom, standing watch. I was fixated by their beauty. I dare not move or they might go away. After some time my eyes grew heavy, and I fell asleep again.

Since that experience, I have been asked to describe, what does an angel look like? Not as artists have depicted them in their paintings for hundreds of years. Angels do not have wings and do not fly. Angels levitate. Even if standing, if you look closely at their feet, you will find they are not touching the floor. The second thing, you will notice their bodies give out light. You only need to read St. Luke ch 2 vs. 9, As there were no street lights, it would have been impossible for the shepherds to have seen the angels as they watched over their sheep at night without the light the angels cast.

With my mother's inheritance, [which partly stolen by her brothers, causing her considerable pain, and separation from her family. Later in life I was able to get her to be reconciled to them and to come back into the family fold, much to my and her own gratitude. It was this very example that showed me that if you fail to forgive others' who sin against you, then the hurt you feel is yours alone, and does not to the same affect on those who sinned against you]. We could at last buy our own home, as opposed to renting.

My father had been a church warden, as had my grandfathers also, and all were well known. Later when Rev Geoff Schurr was forced through ill health to leave Shirley. My father told us one evening, that Bishop Warren, wished to place in Shirley a young man, had asked dad, at their first meeting to find a new vicar, that the Bishop had some one in mind for Shirley but the person the Bishop had in mind was young and the Bishop saw dad as this person to provide this help for the new vicar, as dad had many years as a warden in two different parishes.

After we had chosen the new home, I awoke to find a man in my bedroom. He said to me, "Do not be afraid, I am Jesus of Nazareth". I am not sure of His exact words beyond this point, but in essence, God The Father was guiding my father in the search for a new home of their own, because they would contribute much to Shirley, and I also would learn a lot from a boy of my own age to act as a mentor for me.

My secondary schooling was less than a year old and when we went to visit a possible home we passed by a house of a school friend and he came to me on the Monday, to enquire why I had been observed passing his parents house, and I started a friendship, with a twelve year old Ross Elliott. Christ never told me my mentor's name but I would soon discover him. I was new to the area very immature, and Ross knew those older who would guide him into The Christian faith, I was also in Bible Class with Ross and I would follow the same path to becoming a Christian. Canon Acheson the vicar was the powerhouse for all this development. His only living relation was Dean Acheson Secretary of State in the Eisenhower government in the United States. One of these ladies, Ann Lincoln was to become principal at a Maori girls high school Te Waipunamu College.

Ross the next year introduced me to Crusaders, which I had not heard of previously, where we studied St Lukes Gospil. I thought having someone to guide my actions sounded a bit far off, so I told no one, but I now had Ross in Bible Class in church and once a week also at lunch time at school. The leader, coming into school on a voluntary basis, establishing Crusaders to teach Christianity.

Much later in life I attended Walter Hurst's funeral. All Wellingtonians would have known him through his daily newspaper columns. Archbishop Brian Davis delivered the eulogy. I never forgot his words. Apparently Canon Acheson had spoken to Walter Hurst back in Ireland to encourage him into the ministry, and to come out to New Zealand when his studies were over. Walter's first church as a vicar was in Taranaki, where he arranged the first Bible Study group for older boys and girls in the region and took this himself. Archbishop Davis was thinking of an office job until Rev. Walter Hurst suggested to Brian Davis, if he had considered taking Holy Orders, so now I stand before you as your Archbishop. I never forgot that moment. You can see for yourself how a suggestion can with God's help lead into new avenues of thought. Canon Acheson's suggestion taken up and onto others.

Canon Acheson, died shortly opening of the new Stephen's, and we had the pleasure of having as our fill in vicar and a friend to Canon Acheson, Rev F Vivian Fisher, the first vicar I ever knew, whom I had a great deal of respect for. Now I could reconnect back, and our family became again regular visitors to 23 Slater Street.

Our new vicar was Rev. Geoff Schurr, who started his career as an engineer for in an air craft factory in Britian. His father had died and his mother remarried. His step-father was the first Anglican Bishop of Jerusalem. He influenced Geoff to go to Oxford to be trained as a minister. Geoff was very proud of having won an Oxford blue for rowing. I knew Rev. and the second Mrs Schurr for over 30 years.

After six years as our vicar, Geoff had a long illness. I had promised Rev. Schurr, I would teach Sunday School, once I had completed my own studies at University.

It appeared to me that God had changed His mind, as I heard nothing more for about nine years. What was all the fuss and attention from God concerning myself all about? I decided to try and find out. I added to my normal readings and prayers a request to finding answers. Why was there all this silence. This I asked at least three times a day, and in the latter up to seven times. By now my mentor, Ross had gone to Wellington or Auckland to further his own studies in engineering and my own life had matured, as my belief had grown.

The day had arrived for the service for possible union with the other denominations at which Rev. Schurr would deliver the sermon. He had a long recovery, with Archdeacon Gowing [later Bishop of Auckland] making various pastors available to take our services and speaking to dad to let him know who was appointed to take the services on Sunday. Rev. Schurr thought he would have plenty of time in his recovery to do this task.

Dad thought, if we left early, we would not have to search for a parking place and run ourselves late. St Columbia's Presbyterian, was where the combined service in Petre Street was to be held. Unlike most Presbyterian churches, St. Columbia had only two rows of pews, much like Anglican churches. Our family sat on the left hand side, four rows back from the front and against the central naïve, with myself against the pew end. Stewards began to bring in extra seating from the hall and fill in any empty spaces for late arrivals and usher them in to the vacant seating. Mother suggested we could pack closer together, so that the pew we sat on would accommodate an extra person. No one occupied the extra space we created, and I began to feel lonely in the crowd.

The first hymn was announced. We stood. A late arrival came in and ushered into the position we had created. He stood beside me and entered the singing. I am 173 cm tall. I estimated he would be 178 cm tall. He was of slight build and looked to be about 30 years of age. At the end of the hymn we were asked to sit and bow our heads for the first prayers. It was a tight squeeze. I could see he was wearing an overcoat. As it was mid-winter this was not abnormal. Most men's overcoats a few years earlier had mostly been grey and these had quickly faded. Most had been discarded. Only the poor had clung to their almost white coats. Perhaps the man next to me was in the poor category.

I began to feel my space was being invaded. Now I began to feel pressure on my left side coming from my mother, and pressure on my right upper arm and also on my right thigh from the corresponding parts of the stranger. My mind began to wander, as I tried to find the reason, as a tingling sensation slowly began to creep into me coming from the stranger. Then I thought of the bible story of the two travellers on the road to Emmaus. I told myself not to be so silly. Jesus would be far too busy to be bothered with a nobody like me. I was just being stupid or over dramatic. The tingling sensation kept on slowly creeping across my body towards my mother.

What could I answer if, she whispered, what are you doing? I must find out who was this stranger, as he must live nearby. There is a chance, if I can recognise him, I may be able to speak to him later. It had not occurred to me earlier to look at his face, so I turned my head a little and opened my eyes to find I was looking at his groin. Bother! I will have to shift my position a little and sit up straighter, but not too much to be obvious. Sitting up a little I was hoping to get a better view of the side of his face. This time I could see his chest. That had not worked either. The tingling sensation had continued and had now claimed almost all my body. How am I going satisfy my mother, if her body begins to also be invaded. I was feeling panic. She will never believe me, should I say "nothing". What else can I do?

Finally, I had to admit. This has to be Jesus, The Christ. Immediately the tingling sensation had gone. The seat was empty. There was no one on my right side. I was left with the pleasure of knowing I had recognised Jesus without seeing His face. I felt that Christ had left me, as if I was standing upon a pedestal. My feet felt they were about 65 cm off the floor. This lasting sensation led me to giving my blessing. MAY YOUR SOUL BE UPLIFTED IN THE PRESENCE OF THE LORD.

I arrived home one evening, just after the Rev. Maurice Goodall, became our new vicar, to find him on our back lawn. I thought he was waiting to see my father, but quickly he said it was me he wished to speak. Then he asked me to consider joining Christian Graduates, who were beginning their new year and to come along with him as I had just recently completed my degree. I went for the next three or four meetings until I got a position in Auckland and transferred there. The

Canterbury Group were to study an essay by J.M. Bailey called, God was in Christ, a very interesting study.

The first big event on coming to Auckland was to attend a youth service for Gladys Alwood, who a few days earlier had been thrown out of China by Chairman Mao, for being a Christian missionary. This was held in the Y.M.C.A. Sports arena. She was on the floor but raised up on a platform for us all the see. She was responsible for getting young girls to have their feet unbound so they could walk more naturally. She read a passage from her bible in Mandarin and then repeated it in English. She told us that when riot had broken out in a provincial jail the governor would loose his position if he could not squash the riot and so he had taken Gladys and pushed her inside the door of the prison. Gladys in fear for her life did not know what to do. She stood quietly and after the prisoners saw her, they ceased, not wanting her seeing their behaviour, and when all returned to normality she was taken out unharmed. What can I say, but you can see God in action.

One of my dreams was in China, and although I later found it was realistic in its details which I had never knew previously, the dream never occurred in my life.

The first Church I attended in Auckland, was St Oswalds in One Tree Hill, where I became a Sunday School teacher. Keeping my word to Rev. Schurr. My class was form 2 boys who had to supply one of their members each month to take the parsons roll in the family service. I think at large they did an excellent job with the morning prayers. I told them not to panic should they for any reason loose their place or could not pronounce a word, as a slight pause, may to them appear as a large gap time wise, but to everyone else it may appear to be no more than just a few seconds.

At a meeting of all the teachers led by the Sunday School Superintendent, she said miracles don't happen now. I was furious inside. If we don't have eyes to see we will never notice God at work. My furry led me to dream the longest dream of my life, taking eight hours or more to complete it is this dream which takes centre stage to the whole of this essay.

The next passage is out of sequence within my life and refers to a much younger Barrie. To my mind I have kept it a little late in telling of this particular dream. It shows The Father in two distinct moods.

I was playing outside in heaven when an angel came and told me that God The Father wanted to see me and took me by the hand. I was approximately ten years of age in this particular dream. I grabbed the hand of another boy who looked rather like my brother of twelve, for I was scarred for my future. A little like being called before the head master at school. When I entered the presence of God I could see a long curved stairway with tongues of flame on each riser. I let the hand of the boy go as the angel also let my other hand go, and The Father indicated that He wanted me to come up to Him. As soon as I took a step up these stairs, The Father stood up from His throne, and fear took hold of me, with my thoughts spinning in my head, as I told myself that not even The Queen of England would stand for me, yet here our God and maker stands.

My past sins, were taken back and became a heavy burden. A weight so great that I stumbled and fell down on the third step while I said, "I was not worthy to come into your presence".

Immediately. God's expression changed from a smiling, happy, and loving father figure into a wild and angry God. His long cloak flowing, His eyes blazing like two laser beams with blue anger, His long hair moving wildly or as Revelation states, 'moving like serpents'. His whole countenance quite blue with rage. The Father points a finger at me, and says, "How dare you call defiled that which I have made Pure and Holy through the sacrifice of my Son".

9

Immediately, realising I had made a mistake, my fear seemed to loose its grip and bravely I stood up and said "I am sorry, but I did not realise the extent of forgiveness" as I felt the burden of sin removed.

The Father's face returned to look kind and loving. His eyes shone with love in a rose red light. A complete transformation. Now I only wanted to get up those steps as quickly as possible. Now that I could see the fullness of the love of God.

I want you to understand the complete forgiveness The Father offers, without the right for you to ever think again of the sins forgiven, because God's sacrifice was one of a Son without sin. Therefore this sacrifice was perfect in every way and in all terms. You are truly forgiven when you accept Christ into your life. That is why Christ is so special and demands all your love. It is this depth of forgiveness, that is your inheritance, on which you must concentrate your mind to accept.

Jesus needs us to give him complete loyalty and love, yet so many of us say, "I am an atheist", I say you are just lazy. Still others say they belong to a different religion, trying to hide from the truth. Where else but God The Father can you turn to and in Jesus will you find complete forgiveness. Nowhere it is a narrow path that you must walk. Acceptance of Christ is the only way that leads to heaven. Stop and look, and ask yourself, who am I?

You can always find time, no matter how busy life appears. Be stopped at the traffic lights, and get into a rage, because you did not get through before the red light. A sure condition for an accident. Perhaps it would be wiser to first to thank God for giving you a moment to concentrate your mind on others, even on God Himself. Just a quick word, and He will give you patience, peace of mind, and make you ready for the journey ahead, calm and collected.

At home on a cold day, forget the children. Find a place of quiet, snuggle up in warmth, perhaps your favourite chair. Now take time for your own being. Look at yourself with a close scrutiny, and a deep understanding what you are looking for. Understand that you are both body and soul. Ask yourself some deep personal questions. Fill the time with having a conversation in your mind with your soul to assist your soul to be alive both to you and The Living God. Stop walking around with half yourself dead. You will see God has a precedence for heartfelt prayer and to talk back through The Holy Spirit, or The Comforter, as Christ calls Him to your soul. So if you have neglected your own soul and starved off the very part of you that has ears for hearing God, how will you hear God calling you? It takes patience. You may have to persist. You may have to continue some time persist and God will answer you, when He knows you are listening.

I read about a South African vicar many years ago, who first thing in the morning opened the blind and then the window and he would call, "Good morning Lord", putting God first. Try, keep on trying until you have to admit you are no longer an atheist, and rejoice to yourself that you have found GOD.

The first Epistle of John Ch. 4. Read it, and try to understand what John is saying. Let the truth of these words impinge upon your total thoughts. I like John, love them because I know The Father. I acclaim them as the truth. They give a true picture of the nature of God. John tells us God is love, and if you love, God loves you and God abides in you, and you abide in Him. How much closer can God get to you without you noticing Him? That is why I tell you that you are lazy. That is why there is no such thing as a holy war. You cannot fight love.

I am telling you this to wake you up to the truth. Not to make you feel guilty. I am also trying to show you my own relationship I enjoy with our God in this essay. I am trying to show you how you also can have a healthy relationship with The Trinity and allow God to rule your life.

My first position, work wise was based in Auckland as an Industrial Chemist. From being a Sunday School teacher, I went to a Diocesans wide meeting for Sunday School Teachers, or at least the city churches. This was taken by a very capable canon, who found himself fulfilling the role of principal of St John's Theological College immediately after the death of the past incumbent. On my way to the first meeting I felt I should reconsider going as most would be oldies, and at just 22 I would feel in the wrong group. It became obvious even before the meeting got underway that my thinking was wrong with about 10% being about my own age group. Almost the last to arrive were a lady, her husband, and their boarder. I knew the boarder, as I had seen him before on a number of occasions. We all were required to stand individually and introduce you to the others. It came to the boarder's turn and he began giving his name and telling us he was a survey cadet before adding he also had a mild interest in athletics. Of course this was the great Peter Snell. A mild interest in athletics, surely an understatement, if ever there was one.

Referring to myself as just a normal human being, however, is no understatement. It is simply the truth.

This all took place just a few months after the Tokyo Olympics, where Peter Snell won his second gold Olympic medal for 1500 metres. The three medalists from Tokyo came on to New Zealand, and had treated us to a repeat performance in Auckland, coming to the tape in exactly the same order. Snell gold, Odazole of Checkoslavia silver and Daves New Zealand bronze.

Much later, about 20 years, Chris Lewis became the first New Zealander to gain a final berth at Wimbledon. He bought a young man, unknown in New Zealand at the time to give him practise and to be able to arrange tennis matches for us to see him throughout the country. The young man in question went on to win his first crown at the New Zealand Open in the following season and went on to become a household name, by winning many crowns in the larger events around the world. He is Borg from Sweden. As I had never seen Chris Lewis in person, only on T.V., and he was to play at Mitchell Street Park, where I played squash; I thought I would go and welcome him home and see him in person.

It was summer and hot, so I wore shorts. I sat in the second row back much closer than would be possible at Wimbledon. I really enjoyed watching Chris Lewis in person playing this match. Later I got up to leave the court, and Chris Lewis chose to come over to speak to me. I was overcome by this generosity on his part. He has a soft voice as I do also making it hard to hear, with all the background noise of people meeting old friends. He had to stand very close. I learnt that his early days of playing tennis, had been at Mitchell Street Park. He impressed me a lot, and I still think of him. He was a real gentleman, in my mind and the best sports person we have ever produced. I have had the pleasure seeing many of our top sports people, but none to come up to his level. I would love to know him now and perhaps still be friends.

Now I have digressed enough to give your minds a little digression from the heady material so important for you to take in, and to show you I am just a man like you all.

The Canon who led us into a study of the Anglican Church, which at the time had twelve separate services fashioned along similar lines for different countries within the Anglican Communion. He also required us to perform play roles to get us into the idea that there were other ways the church felt important. Each evening study ended with compline. A very lovely short service, used in monestries every four hours. A different service for each of the six in the day.

The next year I put my name in for consideration, for the ministry. Jesus wanted me to operate outside the established church in my ministry to be more similar to his own ministry, and took my memory away for a period to keep me in check. It was at the interview stage that I first met David Cole also a candidate. He was the only candidate to make an impact on me. I felt the reverse may have been just as true, but losing my memory meant I had to pull out. David followed Bishop Goodall in his later ministry becoming Dean, an then Bishop of Christchurch.

13

Jesus placed a great deal of influence on my actions each time I appeared to branch out in a new direction in order that God's plans would be adhered to and in ways I was not aware.

The next really large activity for me other than continue to remain a Sunday School Teacher was to take part in a passion play, organised by the Catholic Church in Remuera, wanting to contact people who moved away from the established churches. The Catholic Church felt that if all the churches combined, they could all benefit from the results of the survey. The Churches all agreed and the Passion play would be used to increase peoples' interest and become a draw card to the coming survey. The Catholic Church had made contact with a south Canterbury lady who had put on Passion Plays in many different parts of New Zealand and to train the players for a number of years. I was surprised to learn that one of mother's cousins had made all three crosses. The cross for the person to play the part Christ measured fourteen feet long [4.3 metres] so that it could be put into a hole dug down about 3ft 6inches [just over 1 metre]and a wooden wedge placed behind the cross to hold it firm in the ground. Each of the cross's side arms were 7 feet long. [just over 2 metres] The whole cross was made from 10 inch by 1 inch timber being hollow inside. The actor playing Christ for the three falls, was told, that when he wanted to act a fall to lay close to the ground and the cross would fall in a bounce fashion and he would not be hurt. The actor would stand on a small platform. An old square railway nail would be wedged into a square hole on each of the two cross pieces with a few bangs for the actor to hold onto between two fingers on each side.

The thieves would be tied onto their cross beams with rope, and later be lowered down with a long length of cloth placed across the bare chest and behind the arms, so the two persons on these crosses could be lowered down and caught by a strong actor, as the thief fell forward. One night one of the thieves was missed, and I heard the Timaru lady say, "I hope the thief does not get up and walk away", because she happened to be standing close to me in the dark. The thief stayed where

He had fallen. From there he was picked up and taken into the dark before standing. He had fallen down hill and had not hurt himself.

I had talked an English immigrant, who I had met after church, if he would take part also as we were needing a few more players. The Timaru lady made him the second thief and was asked if he had a pair of speedos to hold up the loin cloth which was pinned to his speedos with safety pins. One night he forgot his speedos so the ladies helping to prepare the actors like glue on faulse whiskers were forced to use his underpants. The ladies dressing the players could not get his underwear to work. He was worried and so was I for having placed him in an awkward position, after the ladies had failed. I said I would help him. I turned him to face away from me to avoid putting him in any kind of further uncomfort, then I stretched the top of his underwear tight across his lower abdomen holding this in place with two vertical large safety pins. Now to take up the slack I had to use two more vertical safety pins like pleats. It appeared to work, so I left the loin cloth to be pinned by the ladies and hoped it would work when he had his arms tied with rope to the cross and in the glare from the search lights. I never heard any more so I assumed it was a success.

Our young curate in Remuera, where I was now living, also took part. I liked him a lot, as he had remarked to me on a number of occasions about my enthusiasm for the Christian faith. I have to admit one of my problems in life has been loss of memory and it is not surprising to me that his name now escapes me. I would have wished for a closer friendship with him. It could have done us both good. He was such a lovely person and I long to know him even now at the end of our lives. He also had a great love for football, such that when we were learning our parts and there was a lull in the activity he would get his football and kick it high over the grounds of King's Preparatory School where the Passion Play was to be performed.

There were eight performances. I played the part of Simon of Cyrene, and cum the Monday after I noticed that my arms were heavily bruised, because I had no for-warning when the cross would fall.

I left Auckland for my home in Christchurch, as I needed a complete break. In Christchurch we enjoyed a new curate and his wife, as well as the Rev. Maurice Goodall and a new enlarged Sunday School. It was a wintery day, heavy overcast not a speck of sun and as our curate was consecrating the wine, he lifted up the cup placing a hand above the cup a shaft of light came through the south facing celestial window. [for you northern hemisphere people that is polar facing in the southern hemisphere] The light shaft was directed into the cup. The polished inside of the cup glowed with a strong flash of light. I saw this as a miracle of the power of God. I am sure I am right.

After two and a half years, The National council of Churches in New Zealand held a national conference in Hamilton and they needed team leaders, so I went to Hamilton. Three special trains, and a number of busses bought the youth of the country to Hamilton and they appeared to take over the City with all the government schools being used as dormitories, and the old Agricultural and Show buildings close to the centre of Hamilton being the venue for the combined meetings and for feeding the attending youth.

The various denominations held services each evening, so that we could experience the variety of services being offered. Here I met my friend from Auckland Bruce Owen, who had bought his car and could assist with transport. Bruce only wanted to go to Anglican services, so I was unable to experience the services of other Churches like The Society Of Friends.

The leading Theologian and main speaker was Dr. D. T. Niles, from the Methodist Church in Ceylon, now Sri Lanka. A surprise for me. The second speaker was Dr. Nababan from the Batoc Christian Church in Indonesia, a bigger surprise to me because prior to this I knew nothing about there being a Christian Church in Indonesia. An Anglican minister, took charge of the notices and the general organisation of the meeting. Catholics were then not part of the N.C.C. In New Zealand, but had allowed four of their youth to be observers.

When I returned to Christchurch, I had been selected to organise groups of youth in various parts of the city interested in N.C.C. activities. I met a man who had tried before and now wanted to hand on the mantle because he now had a growing family. He suggested we hold a meeting of those committed to this aim at the Presbyterian Church on the outskirts of Christchurch's centre, but wanting to promote members of the smaller Churches to feel they also belonged, I proposed we seek to hire the newly built Salvation Army Cidel and its hall, very close to Christchurch's centre where I had not previously been, in order to make as much as I could for all denominations of all sizes as equal members of N.C.C. My suggestion was accepted and I think, it helped to influence the make up of youth interested in N.C.C. This influence, did not spread to the outer regions of the city as I had wished. In north eastern Christchurch where Shirly is situated there was a different reaction because I had already held a meeting organising all the Churches there to hold a combined youth service, and I had approached Rev. Maurice Goodall, if we could hold it one Sunday evening there. He gave his approval and my part ended there, because there were more than sufficient enthusiastic young people without me to take the whole service and each had agreed on their parts.

The Church of Christ on Morehouse Avenue was represented at The Salvation Army meeting by a number of their youth accompanied with their minister, who made a large contribution with ideas and plenty of enthusiasm. As far as I am aware there was only a youthful Methodist minister who supported his youth. With two to three week prior notice that is bad.

The Church of Christ minister [whose name I cannot remember], stood up and suggested the central group begin with a camp he had pencilled in, to discuss what activities the youth wished to take on. The young Methodist minister told us they had a vacant flat on the banks of the Avon near to Columbo street which they would rework and we could use to bring other youth to Christ.

As the initator of this meeting I was asked to also make myself available for the proposed camp. The camp went well under the Church of Christ minister's guidance. We had a cup of tea and a biscuit, as some churches, did not celebrate communion. It was suggested we accept the Methodist Church's offer and to use the flat as an outpost to the youth of the city, for a cup of coffee and a chat about their lives. It reminded me of Ross Elliott inviting young people into the Cathedral to attend a service, while I was busy trying to get a degree.

We got little success at first, but this changed as news spread, they could have a safe meeting place. After about two months, I had to have a Friday night off so I left the older methodist minister's son in charge, but he let the flat to run itself and we had a difficult job to restore it to be effective again. Now I had another decision to make. To accept a position with Shell Oil, or not. It was a step in the right direction for my future employment. After some thought I accepted. A day or two later I received a letter from the Church of Christ minister asking me to offer myself to the N.C.C. for the vacant position of youth leader on the board of N.C.C., but the letter only arrived on the same day as the N.C.C. annual general meeting, and would be over. Also I had to think of my commitment to Shell Oil. There was nothing I could do.

I had never been in Wellington before. I bought a map, but it showed none of the business locations, so to a novice, it was useless. I rummaged about in one of the better bookshops, the first Friday evening, and found the last book showing all the churches, parks and most of the business locations as well describing how to get to a certain street in the city or a suburb in a dictionary of street names designed for taxi drivers. I really liked that little book and wished they could make them profitable again. Running about in a bus with most churches appearing as last century look alikes, unless you happen to be able to see and have the time to read the churches notice board; made finding a place to worship very problematic. Therefore, I made up my mind to attend the partly built new cathedral. I was welcomed with warmth and to me it felt like going home instead of attending a service amongst some of the elite of New Zealand society. I could hardly be happier.

Again for some time I became a Sunday School Teacher.

I decided about this time, to join World Vision, and give some aid to a Child. About the same time I heard of children in Brazil from the poorer areas, being shot for trying to find food to keep them alive. If I were rich I said to myself, I would start my own help centre called, 'Come on Inn' and have schooling, food and shelter for the children, with auditors to see the cash was being used wisely, as well as moral auditors to save the children from miss-use. That was not possible. World Vision were in Brazil then. I was given a boy about ten years old from Belo Horizonte, whose wish was to play football. I later was told by World Vision that some people in Brazil were keeping a portion of the donations for themselves, and World Vision were leaving Brazil.

I decided to look elsewhere. I found The Lebanon, whose country was being bombed because of Syria, and Israel, and the Gollan Heights. Whoever was at fault, then it certainly was not the Lebanonese children who suffered through the bombing and the lost of parents and their homes. So I thought to help them. I was given a little girl aged about 9 years. Her name was Salpie. She was a bright little girl and did very well for herself at her schooling. I supported her for about 4 years and I liked her a lot because she had stamina and made every opportunity she was given to improve her-self. I went to an adult education class to learn Arabic so that I could wish her a Merry Christmas without the need for translation. I never heard anything more from her and suspect Israel interfered. I was quite angry.

About two years later, the Anglican Church held a national conference for young people in their twenties at Lincoln University, not so far from Christchurch. Bruce was going so I thought it would be great to catch up with him and I decided therefore, to go also over the long summer holidays.

The main speaker was the Bishop of Guildford, who had previously been the vicar to London's largest city church of 80,000 parishioners. He was quite a wit and his humour was a hit for those in attendance at the conference. He talks in his book in having trouble after an early morning service to having his breakfast, with all the phone interruptions. Exasperated with another interruption he took up the phone and answered, "The vicar in the middle of his breakfast".

Back came the cool reply, "The Bishop, not yet having started His".

His addresses were just as excellent as his wit. He ended his evening addresses with the following verse:-

> The day is over with its lights and shadows;
> The vesper tide shines tranquil in the west;
> Then turn me O my soul from things created
> Unto thy rest.
>
> From vanities and fools and faint endeavours,
> From which, O lord, thou knowest I love thee still,
> The homage of a tired mind I bring Thee,
> And steadfast will.
>
> That all within me, That I shrink from telling
> I yet beneath Thy pitying gaze can stand;
> Stretch o'er me Lord, for healing and for blessing,
> Thy pierced hand.
>
> Hide me as the long night draws ever nearer
> With every hour of this life's lessening span:
> Thou hast tasted death, immortal Saviour,
> For every man.

Lighten all darkness of the flesh and spirit;
Keep me from fears and perils of the night;
Who of this world and the golden city
Art the true light.

Thou dost give Thy very self Lord Jesus,
For those who seek the things above,
What less than self-surrender dare I offer
Thine awful love?

With angels and archangels and blest spirits,
Who to the Triune God their hymns address,
We praise Thee and adore in solemn gladness
Thy Holiness.

The morning lessons and addresses were given by Canon Peaston from Christchurch Theological College, who later went to Canada. I cannot recall his exact words which he used to open his studies, but it was along the lines of what I have written here. Stay alert, concentrate on the teaching of scripture we are considering today, that you may become wise unto salvation. We all wish for the blessing of God's promise of salvation. My study is endeavouring to lead you into understanding God's promise as much as it is to tell you of my life with the Trinity allowing you to find Christ in your life, finding in Him a deep love bring you into salvation.

The wife of Bishop George Reindorp, Bishop of Guildford was a medical doctor and so they became known as body and soul. One keeping the body in top working order while the other endeavouring to do likewise for the soul. Many jokes were invented along these thoughts. The truth is we are both body and soul and both needs to be fine tuned.

Guildford only became a separate diocese in 1910. In 1960 Guildford saw the young Queen Elizabeth and her Duke come to the consecrations of the new cathedral. Lay people had been hard at work making items for the cathedral, including new investments. One lady got a bit carried away in her efforts to impress when she produced a new mitre for the bishop. The bishop says she had forgotten about the strong winds and the mitre's large size made it hard for the bishop to control. Bishop Reindorp remarked on this difficulty as he was leading the Queen and Duke out of the service and had to make a quick snatch to catch the mitre as it became airborne.

The Duke of Edinborough replied, "You are lucky, I had to hire my outfit".

We all spent part of one day on a trip to Akaroa, The French settlement on Bank's Peninsula, where some of our group found an old whale pot [historical ornament] on the beach. Someone suggested the Bishop get in for a photo-shoot, when another group found a small piece of paper rubbish and put this under the pot lighting the paper for a more realistic photograph.

Bruce and I hired a car fot two days after the conference, and drove into the foot hills of the Southern Alps. We stopped in Rangiora for a few moments to see the now retired Rev. Geoff Schurr and Mrs Alice Schurr. We then drove to Kaiapoi to buy Fish and Chips, stopping beside the Waimakariri River to eat them. The river was high in flood. I had never seen so much water in the river before, soil laden with large waves reaching up to just below the bridge decking. Then two young farmers in a Hamilton jet boat came past us and turned to come to the Waimakariri river's bank and offered us a ride of our lives, one at a time, so that the protective gear they carried could be used for each of us, one at a time. Bruce was on the first trip and I on the second. We had to don a life jacket and stand holding onto the supports to the windscreen because the force of the water would bounce any person off their seat, if you sat down. I had to take off my sunglasses now covered in drying muddy water in order to see. The water was just filled with mud. The intake for the jet was below the bottom of the boat, therefore, when the bow and the stern were both in water the centre of the boat was not in water, and being suspended the boat stopped until the intake for the water reached the top of the next wave. It was a crazy ride, but a great experience for us both.

Now back to our topic. Having returned to Wellington, I was on a trip to Palmerston North, taking the short way through Shannon. This road has hills and many turns, so it is essential to keep focused on your driving. I knew I had a lump on the side of my neck because my doctor had spotted it, which I had not previously. Now the lump began to pain me. What could I do? I thought if I prayed and it did not work, then I would not allow failure to affect my faith, so I prayed with my eyes wide open looking ahead along the road, that Christ would make the strong pain subside. Immediately I prayed for relief, not only the pain went, but also the lump, which I had had for a number of months. The fingers of one hand tried to find the lump with the hand on the opposite side on the wheel while driving a straight piece of road. The lump had completely gone as well. I wanted to jump for joy, but driving I could not. What else I enquired in my mind? So keeping my eyes fixed on the road ahead, all that was possible for me was to say quietly. "Thank you", to Christ. Somehow, I also came to the realisation, I had also been granted healing hands. This was the first time for me to use this power.

After this I experimented with using my hands for healing with both positive and negative results. A bit like trying a bicycle for the first time, keeping your fear under control in case you fall off.

An Anglican vicar introduced a group of us in using anointing oil, but for me it had no effect. Laying on of hands for me appeared the best approach. Then we were introduced to holding a special evening meeting to give those who had a concern and those who felt they could use prayer for assistance. Then a lady from our church one evening came and asked for help. Her son-in-law who was not a Christian, had been told by his doctor and the doctor's colleagues with whom his doctor had put the problem to for a combined opinion, that was nothing they could do for him. The children needed their father, if they were not to be left destitute. Could someone please pray. No one did. I said to myself, I do not have the right to judge others; that is God's right. I decided to pray for her son-in-law's recovery. He was already in a coma she had told us.

The very next Sunday, after church she came to me and told me that as far as she was able to calculate that within the hour of my prayer for help, her son-in-law had begun to be aroused, and by the next morning he appeared well again. To this day I have never set eyes on him. I took the lady into a small corner and gave thanks to Christ, for His healing powers.

This is a new and completely different aspect to my life, I now want to focus upon. Look this is not an area that I can tell you everything. I am unwilling to elaborate where knowledge is unavailable. The service came to where prayers are normally offered. The parson was in a bother because no one had noticed, he stumbled along and then asked it anyone in the congregation had a prayer that we could all share and invited us for assistance. Lots of thoughts came flooding into my mind, like a jigsaw of mixed phases. I would require a pencil and paper to arrange them into an intelligent prayer. I knew the prayer would be a very powerful statement, which would benefit us all if offered up. I decided, I could not put it together, so I would not even attempt doing it, as I had neither pencil, paper, nor time, so I listened to another member of the congregation. I listened closely and recognised his voice. Then the next member began to pray for us and I listened. The voice seemed to be saying someone else had an opening similar to the words I had thought about, and I became uncomfortable, that I had denied others of not offering it myself. I listened harder and Shock! A real jolting shock. It was my voice being used to say these words. I recognised the Holy Spirit had taken charge. I waited for the break between the opening and the body of the prayer, so I could whisper to The Holy Spirit, or as I prefer to call Him, The Comforter. The name The Lord gives to Him, "I can't do the body of the prayer. I'll will have to leave it to you, while I concentrate my thoughts on the completion".

I listened to my voice, being under the control of the Comforter, while I worked on the words of the ending. The Comforter did not let me down. I knew no one in the congregation would believe this was a miracle if I had tried to tell them, yet to me it was more than a miracle, it was the mind of God, The Comforter, interacting with the mind of a man, myself. Quite a quirky feeling. I think I have just made a new word from the word queer which seems to have taken on another meaning, nothing like the feeling I am trying to describe. Laugh, yes but surely you can see God at work again.

Now back to my own actions. I had returned to Christchurch to retire. One day I read in the newspaper, that a young man had escaped from Glorivale Christian College with only the clothes he was wearing, and picked up by a deputy headmaster of a Christchurch school, and bought into the city. The Salvation Army gave him temporary accommodation, at the Army's old mens' home in Addington. I thought I had plenty of rooms which were empty, therefore I could offer him one free for eight months, but he would need to get a small job to pay for the food he would consume.

Eight months, became five years. First I contacted the immigration department, who put me in touch with an Indian Lady, working with immigration for her countrymen. She had arranged for him to take a course in agriculture and plant husbandary and arranging for a scholarship for him so that he did not have to pay for the course, and then she came to see what I was offering to him by way of accommodation.

I did not know how, having been treated like a slave, this had affected him. Losing his teenage years to hard work. I use the word 'slave' for there is no other way to describe his condition. Taken from a mud hut, without privacy and been made to work from 3 am to bring in the cows to 6 pm seven days a week with his keep, and little else. On top of that sharing a room with 8 bunks. The room measuring only 3 metres by 2 metres. I would find it hard to think of any other description. Christian lacks an education in the broader sense, yet he is not without a high degree of intelligence and has a good singing voice. I asked through the government for compensation for him. I was told Helen Clark, as Prime Minister said deport him back to where he had been taken. How heartless to treat people this way, and Helen Clark wants the position in U.N. of General Secretary. I think U.N. should say No! Her answer was to make Christian want to take his own life and put an end to his misery. I had never been placed in a worse situation in my life. I did not know what to do. I was unprepared for that.

Christian had not been to the gym at the time, which he later rectified. Physically he was not strong and I was able to put my arms around him and hold him tight so that he was restricted in his movement and could not go and do anything stupid. I told him I would intervene on his behalf if necessary. Christian has never done anyone any harm. His honesty is unbelievable. I have tried to treat him as a son. He is now a New Zealand citizen and all New Zealand should be proud to have him amongst us. Christian gave me a great honour when he said, "You are the only white person he knew that has never treated me by the colour of my skin, and never thought that he was any different to you"; to me that was just lovely.

The longer time, and the need to provide him with the decencies of life, resulted in my loosing my home. I think it would be approximately three years with a lot of hard times and work to be able again to think of buying another home. I know Christian still needs my help, and my intensions are still to aid him as much as I can.

I promised Christ, lying in bed when Christ came to me to write down all of my life, with The Trinity, so it could be common knowledge, and not keep it all to myself. First, I had to remember as much as possible. I was resolved to tell only the truth, so I could no longer hide behind non-disclosure to achieve a normal life, yet I am only a normal person in truth. That has been hard when I had tried deliberately to forget, and it has taken many attempts. Finally trying to write it in chronological order has been the key to this study.

With all my difficulties, followed by the Christchurch earthquakes made me want a new attempt at retirement. I was resolved to seek a new beginning. I also needed to find out if Christian could cope without my help and I knew he did not want to leave Christchurch, therefore by deciding to come to Nelson where my parents had lived about 20 years previous, I could watch from a distance. After the move it has not been all a bed of roses either. I hope the end of my struggles are near and my final assistance to Christian will truly set him free.

This chapter has to be one of excitement for all Christians. It answers questions. It gives you the inside story. It makes me and I hope you also want to clamber, for the love of God. So let us get started. For me, it is more than hope, it is the excitement of heaven, all made possible, when you come to accept God, receiving His love and atonement; and the future you will enjoy when you accept God into your life and become a child of God. I am really surprised, many have read of the event in their Bibles and never thought about the questions the Bible imposes.

The Father in heaven was worried about His Son, such that He called the angel that was selected to become part of me, and is now my soul, to go on a mission for God The Father. The angel knew nothing of what happened on earth. This angel was given a parcel with instructions where God wanted his angel to go. God's aid was the light of God showing the way. God also wanted answers to His questions, and His angel should not hesitate along the way and return speedily. It was around 2 am. In Jerusalem, and pitch black, there being no street lights. It was the early morning, the dawn of the first Easter. The light first took the angel into the Temple in Jerusalem, to The Arc of the Covenant by God's light where the Angel took the presence of God from it to take it back to The Father, as directed by God as He told the angel, soon there will be a new presence which will be within all believers, where ever they may be, for each of them, not just in Jerusalem.

The second part of the mission, was to allow the same light to guide God's angel to where Jesus had been laid. My soul was still belonging to the angel, as a result the angel could levitate above the stones upon which the angel could otherwise trip on his way to the tomb. The Tomb was leaking great quantities of light through the porous limestone from which it had been carved, and so it would have been difficult for anybody awake to miss seeing it. On finding the tomb the angel simply went through. Inside there was no body, for Jesus had already discarded it. The tomb looked just as the disciples and others first gave witness. Its smell was of newly cut limestone telling us that Joseph of Aramathaea was correct in saying the tomb had only recently been completed. It is time now to look at the evidence of the crucifixion. The Romans had killed the mortal man, but they knew nothing of the soul of man, and if they had of known they had no way to destroy it. Those who had laid Jesus in the tomb could not have dreamed that the body would require everyday clothes, and left none. The Father had given His angel a parcel containing the clothes and sandals Jesus was wearing, when those who saw Him testified He wore after the resurrection.

We are now beginning to understand the truth of Easter. I doubt if Christ would have permitted His angel friend, whom He loved above all others, would be granted to have seen The Soul of Christ naked, but His angel had been given special eyes, not to have been blinded for this special moment. Both Jesus and His angel were and are very much friends. The inside of the tomb was blinding bright. Did not Jesus say, "I am the light to the world".

I wonder what would have happened, if His angel visitor had seen the earthly body after the crucifixion probably fainted, for the angel did not know what to expect. The angel sensed the prescence of Christ in the light and treated it as his friend, giving the light the messages from the Father, including the parcel which the angel laid down between the neatly folded clothes, telling the light that He was very much loved by The Father, and also by this angel. He finally told the light The Father would send other angels to roll away the heavier darker and denser stone blocking the entrance. The angel attending Christ told the light that The Father required the angel's return as quickly as possible, and picking up what he had laid down from the Arc of the of the Covenant again re- assured the light of his love for Jesus, before departing in the same way that he had arrived.

Finally we must look at the Bible description and look at the evidence of events the Bible gives. Christ apeared and disappeared, He also went through walls. All things we cannot do, but spirits can do. Evidence that Christ after the resurrection, is not in a human body but in a heavenly body. We must conclude that the resurrection that Christ performed was a spiritual resurrection into a heavenly body. This is a spiritual awakening. It is a lot to take in, for our minds to accept, but it is important to the overall understanding.

We must conclude that Easter is entirely a spiritual event, and as such there is nothing in this event for non- believers, and much more than we understood, or were told previously for all believers. I personally feel, it strengthens our ability to deeply love The Lord. Praise The Lord!

Before I had received the Easter message, I went to a political meeting, held by the Eastbourne section of Trevor Mallard's Eastern Hutt Electorate, in an attempt to get approval from the area of all the churches in the section for the government's wish to ratify the United Nations agreement on human and family ownership. I spoke at the meeting and found all the churches were in agreement with what I had to say, except for Trevor Mallard who was completely taken aback. I had not thought about the subject previously and I had to think on my feet. Later I came to the conclusion, that this was the first major intervention by God into my thoughts and I should not think so smug when the thoughts were not really mind in the first place.

I said, No one owns you, except God who created you and yourself. Should you marry, you give yourself to your partner, as your partner also gives themselves to you, without exchanging ownership, which you cannot give or receive. If the partnership produces children, then as part of the parent relation each parent has a duty to their children to nurture and educate them as best as they are able to give their children the ability to accept the responsibility of self ownership, along with God their creator.

Understanding the Trinity. I have a little book written by Tom Rees called, 'The Spirit of life, or life more abundant'. Because I have lost my memory several times, for various reasons, I have had to read it often, and my book is now losing its cover. I would be lost without this book of Tom's.

Years ago, I wrote in my copy, 'Now you have received the fullness of the Spirit, act out your life, by living in the Spirit'. This is the most spiritually important exercise you can attempt and not one that is always easy. It takes constant effort, now that you have received the Spirit into your life from Christ himself.

A pupil asked Tom to please explain simply The Trinity. Tom Rees felt this was an impossible task.

This is the only answer you will ever get from me, but you will need to train your mind, to accept these new thought processes which come from God. You are going to need to think in God's terms. The question is are you up to it. This is the answer the Comforter gave to me, understand and be comfortable with the conclusion.

Ancient civilization, had many gods with limited abilities.
God's commandment tells us you shall have no other gods, but God Himself.
In the minds of man we had not been introduced to The Trinity until we learnt of Christ. Therefore understanding the commandment was never the problem.
The Comforter says in God's mind, The word 'God' is a plural word. Just as we think and use words like 'class', 'group', or 'them' or many others you can think about. The exception with 'God' is as we understand it; it is a restricted plurial. Restricted to a maximum of three. Father, Son,

and Comforter. We won't go into the problem as you might see it that the Comforter is everywhere, and in all believers as well as a person in His own right, but your mind is probably greater than mine.

Now do you understand, or do you find it is still a sticky problem. I wonder.

Last of all is the longest dream I have ever had. Is it this that has bothered you? You will find here a new prophecy. First I feel I need to apologize to Christ for I thought all my experiences including this dream were to educate me of God's plan and was private. Therefore, if I did not have to constantly think of it, I could lead a normal life. Then Jesus came to me and asked me to write all this down, so it would become public knowledge. And I could not hide from it.

After attending one of God's meetings where God tried to put His thoughts to his selected few for consideration and remove mis-understandings, Jesus led me out through the back of the Temple into His favourite garden. I am trying to avoid repetition, rather not telling you what you will want to know. He was in a joval mood having left the meeting. I was left a bit perplexed, and never really accepted what Jesus was saying when he was being quite blunt in telling me of my beginnings. For Him this was a joyful moment. For me I felt a little crushed. A long time before Jesus was born on earth He lived with His Father in heaven and was asked, with whom Jesus would like to share His throne with and Jesus replied God's favourite angel, but God had wanted a human. God asked and received a positive reply from this angel he would accept God's decision, so God would when the time was right, put the angel's soul into a human and so solve both their requests in one birth. I was that person. When God found I had not accepted Jesus joval way God followed up on telling me Jesus had not been flippant. He sent an angel to me carrying the book of Ezekiel and I was told to read it. I was reluctant, because this book came up in my normal readings when I was about twenty years old and I did not like its contents, nor did I understand it. About two weeks later I thought

31

I had best read it again. When I came to the description of the four living creatures, then for the first time the Father spoke to me, not in a dream or when I was asleep, but while I was awake and reading. He asked, "Do you not see?"

I replied, "Just the words as they are written".

God then gave me a shock, saying, "Ezekiel is trying to describe, you speaking with us". This is about a thousand years, before Jesus is born on earth. That is why I fell off the corner of my bed. Immediately, I went to look up my new replaced Bible Commentary. I could see the Lion of Juda was The Father, the lamb was Jesus, The Christ, and the dove was The Comforter, leaving the man to be myself, and I had been introduced to the Trinity when God held discussions to help God get a clearer picture of problems as they arose. In my own case of course, it was the angel who had agreed to have his soul transferred into me at my birth.

It would be some years later that Christ came to me and pleaded for me to tell you all these things. Of course I agreed to do so, but this was the first time I knew that all these things were to be made public, so I needed several years and many attempts to remember all the most important aspects of my relationship with The Trinity. I responded as I have told you. I have made a remarkable attempt this time around. The most glaring omission, is now not being able to name all twenty four elders. They were named by Christ, when He introduced them to me when they received their gowns and crowns at the end of my long dream. Most I had not heard of before. Some may had have a different name from the name we may have heard before.

The long dream begun possibly in Rome. I was unable to recognise where I was, as I have never been to Europe. I was told to elaborate on what I told you and as I began, I heard a whisper from Jesus to be quite as our Father wished to speak, and to use my voice. I was later to realise God the Father would not get so annoyed as He felt, if He could camouflage His annoyance. I trembled at The Father's words; tried to recall them, but never successfully, so I am not going to try.

At the conclusion, I bowed my head and waited for the chop of angry listeners when a strong light came from heaven, and a voice spoke, "Barrie, you have done all that I have asked of you, come to me".

I ascended into heaven, just like Isaiah. I hope that will be the case, as you will be more likely to believe the essential points I am making, and there will be nothing of me left for stupid people to want to venerate. I am just a normal human being who does want or deserve any special attention.

When Jesus first called me, I felt my feet were no longer touching anything solid. Then in a matter of a second or two my body was transformed from being human into a heavenly body and the next moment I was standing at the gates of heaven with Jesus and St. Peter.

St Peter asked me, "How is it that you appear to come and go at will, and you are always met by Jesus?"

I knew nothing of this, so how could answer?

Jesus said, "We are keeping our Heavenly Father waiting," and moved further into heaven.

I was struggling to answer Peter. Then the Spirit of the Comforter came to me and told me what to say. I replied to Peter, "Fear not Peter, for I know Jesus loves you", and with that I quickened my pace to catch up with Jesus.

Jesus enquired, "How did you come with your answer for Peter?"

I replied, "The Spirit of the Comforter came to me".

Jesus nodded knowingly, and I began to understand, how Jesus dealt with the difficult questions being asked of Him prior to His crucifixion, We moved along to a corner where a lady was coming out of her house. Jesus stopped as He turned towards me and said, "Barrie, this is my mother, Mary".

I replied to her, "It is a great honour to meet you, Mary".

Jesus reminded me of the need to hurry. The two of us continued some distance towards God's Temple going along the main road which divides the houses in heaven into two halves. Then Jesus turned right into an alley, followed by another turn or two. Where we were going, I knew not, but just followed. We now came to another house and Jesus knocked and He said, "This is the house of your mother's family." Just as the door opened, for me to observe my mother. She went then to find other members of her family. Then she introduced her father to me, whom I had never met before, for he died in 1929 some eight years before my birth.

My mother's father told me, "It is indeed a great honour you give us, for you have bought Jesus to our home to meet with us".

In fact Jesus had bought me, for I had not known where they lived. Before anything else could be said, Jesus again reminded me that our Heavenly Father was waiting for us. We must not keep Our Father waiting. We turned towards God's Temple. It dominated heaven, but was still some distance away. Jesus used this time of walking along the straight road, in an attempt to get me to recognise although He was the Christ, He was also man. Of course I knew this fact and accepted it. What I did not realise was, He was wanting to forge a much stronger relationship with me and all mankind. A closeness which is difficult to both understand and explain. I think that in reality we do not bond to Christ as we should. Given the opportunity of living and breathing the same air does something to you that draws you closer to Christ. It is all within His divine nature as I think of the First Epistle of John and wonder am I reading enough into it, to satisfy Christ.

I am not saying, I don't love Christ, because I know the sacrifice He made and in Him alone there is complete and perfect atonement for all sin; therefore the opposite is the truth. I love Christ more than I can tell. It is just the perfection Christ seeks from me is not as complete as both would wish. Without atonement from Christ freely given when we ask, I would remain a sinner, but with Christ's atonement which Our Father requires of us, I like many others are set free from our past sins. I think we need Christ first as part of The Trinity so that we are enabled to accept His perfect sacrifice. Then we will see the man, in Him.

It has been a deep discussion I know. I need Christ, and you must need Him also for there is no other forgiveness. Remember, also Jesus knew what He had achieved without using His divine powers, and wants the same from us. I know having spoken with Christ so often I also know the sound of His voice. The statement, I have just given you, is the whole basis of what Christ is saying to us all. It is the bottom line of what we can judge our performance upon, and that is a very high line, where I fall down and quite likely the same fate for all of us.

Now we were closer to the Temple's main entrance, I could see the angels on guard. Other angels were inside, so I knew without Christ with me, I would not have been allowed to enter. Still other angels were practicing for singing to God. A large white light similar to an aurora, could seen in the middle of the Temple, hiding God's presence from all eyes. It hung like white sheets, not green from the oxygen in our atmosphere, but white. [There were no windows in God's Temple to let in the light. The Temple being lit from inside; bathed from inside in God's Holy Light created from His presence within. The large doors around the circumference, between the strong pillars, appeared to be sufficient for ventilation, or otherwise it was hidden from my view.] We stepped forward along the naïve. It appeared almost endless for a good half an hour, when we finally came to a region with a raised floor like a platform upon this stood God's throne. Now my eyes had changed, and the original strong white light was no longer an obstacle preventing me from seeing God seated upon His throne.

Standing at the same level as Jesus and myself was a man, and Jesus crossed to meet him. Then I was introduced to the Comforter. We now followed the Comforter to the right side where some steps existed joining the floor to the dias. It was a short quick trip, not giving me time to comprehend all the architectural complications that seemed to arise. We mounted the steps led by the Comforter.

The Father rose from His throne to greet us. First to Christ He spoke a few words of welcome and then the Father put his arms around Christ in a bear hug. The Father was smiling and full of love for Christ.

Now The Father turned towards me, and received me in a similar manner, with a bear hug, and taking a deep breath, breathed over me as He said, "Barrie, receive my spirit in its fullness, for you are going to need it". We were led now to four chairs, and so began our deeper conversation.

As the conversation, led by The Father became deeper and deeper towards The Father's desires for the future, I progressively became further lost in understanding as to what were The Father's intentions, because the limits of human understanding had been stretched to breaking.

The Father realising that I was lost asked His Son Jesus if He felt if He, God, was entering beyond human capacity to understand. Jesus gave this question a long and thorough examination before answering in the negative at which point The Father cosidered what He would do, and came to the conclusion, that He could not change His will, and further thought needed to be given to the issue. This concluded our current discussion, and God The Father adjourned the meeting with Jesus and I leaving.

I am returning to the garden behind the Temple where Jesus had tried to explain to me my life, and the Trinity's association with me. The garden was small when compared to the enormous size of the Temple, but that does not mean it was not large. We entered through a door at the back of the Temple. I could see no edge to the garden. It was here that Jesus went to re-charge His life. Relaxing. Being in His own element with nature. The perfume of the flowers floating about, and the butterflies making the best of the day in their bright colours. That was the reason for His joval attitude which led to me not being sure if He was trying to tell me the truth or just joking. He also asked me what talent I would like to be given. I think He was thinking of wisdom, but I had replied with healing hands. Then Jesus had said in His Laugh fashion, "That you have already been given, in fact you can do so in your own name".

I was shocked and stunned. It took a few moments before I was able to reply. "No, Lord, I only want to heal in your name, that you may have the glory. It is enough for me to abide in the light of your glory." This answer was given before I had my dream of Easter. A long time later I went to a luncheon with some of my old school friends. Patricia who had sat opposite to me in English, and when Ross Elliott, came back from Kenya on leave we met in Patricia's home one evening, and Phylis was also at the dinner was with her husband, back from Africa as well. It was Phylis's Husband who invited me to their table. He is Rt. Rev Henry Poulson who had retired in Christchurch. Bishop Henry introduced me to a walking group in Christchurch where we all travelled about trying to find ourselves in areas of the city I had never sceen. He was a good listener and when I was trying to resolve some forgotten incidents of my past life, I would tell them to Bishop Henry Poulson, often just in the telling would bring back my memory.

Jesus had known my spirit when I had been an angel for a very long time. As an angel I had always wanted to please His Father and worked with diligence, tireless to that end, because I could see The Father's love and wanted to do everything I could to return that love. I had said I will be with you if you are with God and against you if are not and it was obvious to Christ that was my only wish. When Christ told me that my make up was a soul of an angel and a normal body from two God fearing people, I felt my knees becoming week, or as you say today 'My wheels had fallen off '. I was speechless. I wanted to protest, but The Father had gone to such trouble, how could I?

God asked His Son, if He would permit His mother, Mary, to become one of The Twenty Four Elders.

Jesus said, "I want you to see me as both the Spirit of My Father, as well as the flesh of my mother. This acknowledgement drives us apart. Therefore I cannot accept this honour for my mother, if I cannot enjoy the same for Barrie's mother".

The Father accepted Christ's wish saying, "Few women, will serve her God as Violet".

My mother was a Sunday School Teacher, for about ten years. She led the womens group for over ten years, at our church, she worked for 8 or 9 years to raise about one sixth of the cost of a house each year on her own to repay the diocesan loan. Others also raised monies in groups. Mother did her bit alone. When I left home, my bedroom was used by visiting clergy for accommodation. A missionary, on her retirement came first to Shirley to assist the parson, before we had a curate, until with no family of her own decided to join the Sisters of Mercy, an Anglican monastery, where she made communion bread. On her day off, she often came to chat with mother, who would go and pick bunches of flowers for Sister to take back for her family at the monastery.

This was going a bit far. I had not been consulted, then I heard the voice of the Comforter, saying that God The Father needed twenty four elders. All of them will be human. You should calm down and think, as I was near to exploding. I could no longer see if it mattered to me or not, so I said nothing. I did not even tell my mother about this proposal as she was still alive, because I wanted the same surprise for my mother, as all the others. All I ever said to her was that mother was the real matriarch that held our family together.

My father had spent most of his working life, working for the church as well in his daytime job. When he retired, wanting something new to do he joined Red Cross and all his abilities culminated in being made a life member.

I thought at the time that I don't need to tell anyone, so my normal life I expected would remain; without others wanting to interfere, not knowing that I was really telling the truth. Then Jesus came to me a long time later requesting I write it all down. I feel callous that in not believing Him, I have caused Jesus to be hurt as there is no one whom I love more, and at the time I did not read His intensions as He expected. Sometime after the event, as I have already told you The Father gave me a verbal reprimand, showing how Ezekiel also missed the truth of God's message thus keeping us from seeing the Trinity, and man's close association with God.

Sometime later, I hesitate to add the word 'long', Because I will never know the time, but I was again in conversation with The Trinity God, listening to what The Father was saying to us when I began to cry. The Father stopped and enquired the reason for my crying. I told them it had come to my notice that a war was being raged, and amongst other things some were making out that I was more than a man. I told The Trinity, that I had never suggested that I was anything of the nature these people suggested. I had been steadfast in describing myself as a normal human being filled with your Holy Spirit.

The Father then replied that I would not be here, with The Trinity, if ever I claimed more. I should stop crying because the war was now over, and Jesus needed to go and claim His own, and I want you to go with him and provide Him with some extra help in collecting all together for Christ's judgement. You will take this case and open each compartment, only when I command you. We left walking the road from heaven to earth. Jesus dressed in a white simple garment and I walked out of the Temple and past all the now empty houses in heaven to go through the gates and along the road which went down to the earth. Quite a long time after I wrote the description of this road's existence; I found in reading Isaiah this same road. You will find it in Isaiah Ch. 9. The earth looked as if it had been destroyed by fire and was completely devoid of any life.

Jesus now requested that I assist Him to gather all the people together at Mt Sinai. The next moment I appeared as if I was seated in an aeroplane, but there was no plane. I stopped along the way to collect all those who were newly risen from their graves. About half way into this activity, I came to the place where my own family lay burried. The ground opened like it had in all the other places, and the spirits arose. My family were most surprised to see me, as to them, I appeared to be quite impressive. My mother went to embrace me. I was, much to my own surprise, to find myself, motivated by the Spirit saying, "Do not cleave to me, for you have not yet ascended to The Father". I never really understood this saying, or what it might have implied.

I continued to say, "We have no time to waste, as we must go and meet with The risen Lord. I know Him well so you need not fear. To all who know The Lord, you will find Him kind and loving".

Along the way I met the devil, who requested me to open the case, so we could share the contents.

My reply was, "I already have more of the Spirit within me. More than I will need, but I also have the love of God The Father, and the love of Christ and the love of The Comforter. Somethings that you cannot give to me. I need nothing from you". This reply mirrored my thoughts and feelings completely.

The devil now tried to make my burden greater than my strength, so I prayed to my friend, The Comforter, asking Him to give me whatever

I would require to more than equal the demands the devil might place on me, and the devil departed.

Once I had collected for Him, all the spirits, Christ had asked me to collect, I returned making my way to meet Christ. There was such a huge crowd already gathered by Christ, it was almost impossible for us to alight. I thought about the practicality of being able to find The Lord Jesus in this very large crowd. I was on the point of panic, when I heard Jesus The Christ saying, "Barrie".

I turned to see Jesus' wonderful face. Written all across his face was a deep concern and anguish, because of the judgement He knew He was about to perform. Such was this facial expression burning into my thoughts, that I wanted my whole self, to somehow to share His agony. It hurt me to know that was impossible. I am going to break into this description of the judgment to give you a challenge, if you are already a dedicated Christian. You see while you are alive on earth, and it is your wish to take some of the concern and anguish from the Son of God; then each person of your family, friends, or workmates that you can bring to God is one less person for Christ to have to condemn at the judgment. It is your turn to work for Christ.

God The Father then spoke to me, requesting me to open the first compartment of the bag, I carried, where I found a crimson cloak, and following God's instructions, I took the cloak and put around Christ's shoulders. Christ now turned towards the crowd standing before him, and lifting up His arms, spoke His judgement upon them. Those He knew not fell into a gaping hole of fire and some red and others white hot rocks, which had suddenly appeared upon the mountain in front of us. It appeared as a huge split in the darkened earth. Christ now took off the cloak and dropped it onto the ground. As the cloak hit the ground it appeared to liquify, as if it were blood which soaked into the earth.

God The Father, now commanded me to open the second compartment, from which I took a white cloak embroidered in gold. This I placed on

Christ's shoulders and drew the front edges together. I also took white gloves and placed these on His hands. Jesus looked much more familiar to me dressed like this. I am not sure now but there might have been white shoes also.

Jesus now took similar garments, and placed these on me much to my surprise. We stood facing each other with the open case at one side of each of us and took similar garments out as those who were saved and gave them to each person before they began their long walk up the road back into heaven. When all had gone, Jesus stood before me and said, "My friend we must hurry, for there is a long walk ahead of us, before we again meet Our Father and He awaits our arrival". He was my friend and I loved as a close friend, as well as my Saviour...

Both Christ with me at His side entered the gates of heaven, which had begun to close behind us, and no one was there to greet us as Peter had taken His place walking in the possession towards The Temple of The Father. Some already had arrived and taken their seat and now awaited the Lord, The Christ. I turned slightly, and I could make out that even the walls were beginning to encompass the gates of heaven so that they would be no more.

We continued to walk along the the road dividing heaven into two halves towards God's Temple in the possession. All the houses were now empty as their occupants were now seated in the great Temple, or were in the possession slowly making their way towards The Temple. Finally we arived and still had the long walk up the naïve to the centre of The Temple. At last we arrived at the side of The Comforter. God The Father now took control of the proceedings and stood up. It is here that my observations differed from Revelation. I realised I was standing on a blue carpet, not water. I wondered if carpet was a later development, or was it just the enormous size.

The Father asked Christ to kneel at the kneeler placed in front of God's throne, but on a level about a metre lower. Then The Father asked me to open the last compartment, and to take from it a golden cloak with a golden fur edging and I placed this over Christ's shoulders. The comforter was now asked to take from the dias the golden crown of The Spirit and to give it to me to place on the head of Christ. I had never crown anyone before, so remembering the film made at Queen Elizabeth's coronation, I thought to lift the crown high for all to see. As I raised the crown above my head I could feel the crown crushing me, and thought quickly about that idea. I hesitated. Then I gently placed it down on the head of Christ. Now The Comforter was asked by the Father to kneel where I had previously stood to pay homage to Christ now King of Heaven for Himself and The Father. Now I should do the same for all humanity that Christ was truly the King of Heaven. After I was about to stand up after this final act, I noticed that Christ's new golden cloak had become entangled with one of his feet, and if he were to stand, Christ could trip, or worse tear His new cloak. Therefore I whispered for Him to give me a moment to lift His lovely new gown off His foot, in the process almost placing my chin on Christ's knee. I thought, how close we have been at times, and are now, which shows true concern for one another.

Now I straightened myself and holding Christ by the elbows in order to assist Him to stand, I gained the first view of The King of Heaven. I tried to stand to one side to enable His Father to see His Son. Christ's appearance had completely changed. I knew you would want a description. My mind just could not think, as I tried to find words to describe what I could see. I was defeated. Then I said to myself, "If you can describe perfect love, you are also describing the new face of Christ.

God The Father now delivered another blow to my now fragile mind. I thought we had just witnessed would be the end to this great service, not just the first half. How wrong was I? The Father was telling me to kneel at the same kneeler that Jesus had been kneeling. If the kneeler had been further away from me to be able to get some support I would have nothing to hold onto. I am sure I would have crashed to the floor. Jesus now pealed off his golden gown, while still wearing it so that it had become two, and placed this over my shoulders. Now He proceeded to take off His crown while still wearing it so it also became two, and placed the newly formed crown onto my head. Both Christ and The Comforter knelt before me, one after the other, saying they would aid me every way I required, should I ask, to fulfill my pledge to God Our Father.

Now it was time to crown each of the twenty four elders. The night of this my longest dream was fast closing, so there was little time to collect into my memory the names of all the elders, although all the elders were introduced to me individually by Christ. After being introduced I took off my gown, in the same way as Christ had for me and then to repeat the same action with the crown and still had my gown and crown.

Jesus's mother, Mary was the first of the elders, and my mother, Violet was the second to be crowned. There was another ten women followed by twelve men, who all became elders. I was surprised that I found none of the Apostles were among the twenty four elders. Perhaps they did not posess sufficient humility. I had thought to see St Paul and St John, unless Christ used a different names for them.

The Comforter was directed by God The Father to again bring Jesus and myself up onto the dias and while we were doing this, the twenty four elders were each to give the twenty four persons directly behind them a gown and a crown in the same way they had received their gown and crown. Then the newly crowned twenty four who had received their gown and crown each the next twenty four behind each of them and so on until each and every one saved were wearing a gown and crown.

The four thrones on the raised dias were arranged with their backs against a large post holding a canopy above. Christ on The Father's right, and the Comforter on the Father's left. The Father facing towards the main entrance was between Christ and the Comforter. With my back towards the Father's back, the large post being between us. I sat nervously on the front edge of my chair, and looked over the heads of those in front of me. I could see a tongue of flame inside each crown, as it dawned on me, I may have been the first person [human] to have received a crown, I was not alone. Everyone had received the same honour, and I shuffled to sit more correctly, and relaxed. Christ now touched my left arm, to draw my attention to Him. Christ said to me, "I told you I would be with you forever".

My hope is that all will feel free to come and converse as often as you want, and I will introduce to you to The Lord, now King of Heaven. It will be my pleasure.

When Christ turned to face directly in front of His seat, I heard a wind, but there was no wind. Think of the first Witsunday in reverse. The Spirit was been taken from each whom Christ had saved, but the Spirit which was given to us all when we were crowned with the Crown of The Holy Spirit remained, with each of us. The wind slowly grew stronger, as it came together until it was a loud howler and swirled into a new fighter for God The Trinity to achieve the final blow to end the devil's reign, bringing peace to heaven. That person settled high in the canope above us, and is the same person whom Ezekiel thought was God our Lovely Holy Father.

It is my hope and prayer that you will have a new and deeper understanding into The Trinity God, so that you will want to take your studies further praising God the Three-in-one, bringing yourself into true fellowship, becoming wise unto salvation, and receiving God's blessing.

Edwards Brothers Malloy
Ann Arbor MI. USA
January 6, 2017